MW01059624

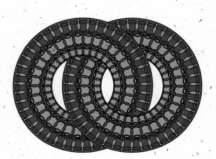

SOUTHERN COMFORT

SOUTHERN COMFORT

Nin Andrews

CavanKerry ⬧ Press LTD.

CavanKerry Press Ltd.
Fort Lee, New Jersey
www.cavankerrypress.org

Library of Congress Cataloging-in-Publication Data

Andrews, Nin.
Southern comfort / Nin Andrews. – 1st ed.
p. cm.
ISBN 1-933880-14-7 (alk. paper)
I. Title.

PS3551.N444S68 2009
811'.54–dc22
2009037300

Cover art Federico Jordan © 2009
Author photograph by Alan Doe

First Edition 2009, Printed in the United States of America

CavanKerry Press is proud to publish the works
of established poets of merit and distinction.

CavanKerry Press is grateful for the support it
receives from the New Jersey State Council on the Arts.

For Suzanne and Jimmy

CONTENTS

Part I   Gills

Part II   Calling the Snakes

Part III Snake Bites

Part IV Strange Birds

Part I

Gills

Powerful Magic

Lord knows it will take a powerful magic to raise you up right, my grandmother from Memphis, Tennessee, liked to say. She always claimed she had eyes in the back of her head. And she was right. Because whenever I did something wrong, she was there to tell me about it. *You did a bad thing,* she'd say. *Yes, ma'am, you did. You did a bad, bad thing. In fact you did a thing so bad, it's a good thing your mama didn't see you. You don't tell her, and neither will I. It will be our secret. Between you, me, and the Lord, Jesus Christ. We don't want to worry your mama, now do we? And we don't want to tell her any bad things.* Then she'd pick me up in her arms and sing me a hymn. I'd lean back to see her lips form the words. I'd watch her bosom rise and fall like waves. Big ocean waves. She'd keep right on singing, too, till I asked her if she was ever going to stop. *Child,* she'd say, *don't you know anything? The Lord's song is never done. You got to make a bad thing good, so sing it. Sing it with me now. Sing it good.*

Cleanliness is next to godliness

Grandma always said.
Most days she met me at the screen door
with a feather duster
or our new Electrolux vacuum,
the hose sucking my blouse.
She said she liked her girls clean.
She said I was coated
with dog hairs, horse hairs,
and God only knows what all else.
Fixing me like a flower bouquet,
tucking in my blouse, fluffing my bangs
and adjusting my barrettes,
she'd stare me down just to let me know
I was allowed in only if she said so.

Indian Summer

It was Indian summer when all the honeybees and wasps came crawling up the walls and window screens. Before my mom could get a grip on her, Grandma had hosed down every bug in our house with Raid. Next she started gathering up the clothes and all the linens in the closets and wardrobes, doing what she called her fall cleaning service. If there was one thing Grandma liked, it was doing the wash. And other things were dead bugs and the Lord, Jesus Christ. But she never did want to be bothered with a clothes dryer. She liked our clothes hung outside, saying the Lord likes honest work, which meant something you did without a socket.

One year it rained so much, our lettuce got slugs and the wilt. My mother said the sheets mildewed. After Grandma took the linens in from the line, they were damp and crawling with daddy longlegs. Mom slipped them in the dryer at dusk, swearing under her breath that Grandma had her ways of dipping into our lives like a pumpkin vine in compost. That year Grandma was reading me her favorite passages from the Bible, mostly about Jesus performing the miracles. I'd sweep the sheets with my fingers, feeling for bug legs. I never could figure how any insect could walk on those legs, thin and wispy as hairs.

Being Mean

It was always Grandma who'd catch me
putting sow bugs in a paper sack
alongside the corn pones and chicken thighs
my mom set aside for Jimmy's snack.
Pranks like that and my sassing folks
whipped her into such a state,
I could hear her in my dreams
alongside the Andalusian rooster
who crowed just about any hour of the night.

When I woke, she was already shaking
her dust mop out on the porch,
telling me a girl like me
best set her heart on the Lord
like a bee on a blossom
and wash her hands and change her trousers
more than once a week.

Sometimes she'd say just as sweet
as syrup, *It sure would be fine*
to have a fresh pot of coffee
and a slice of lemon pecan pie.
She and I would fix a little tea tray.

Sipping coffee and sitting together
on the glider, she'd gaze right through me
as if she were looking through glass
out beyond where the buzz saw droned
and the wild roses bloomed, seeing something
she'd been wanting to forget
a long time. Her sweat
dripped onto the floorboards

while she took up silence
and whittling or sewing a button fly
on an old pair of jeans. I'd fiddle
with the stations on the radio
and peel a dirty Band-Aid off so slow
I couldn't feel a thing.

If I asked what she was thinking
she'd say something short like
There are some things, child,
you'll be sorry you know.
Or: *You think you'll always*
be doing just what you please,

her words circling around me
like barn flies or those mean kids
on the playground I could outrun the days
I was quick enough to see them coming.

Big Foot

When I was a girl, my mother called me Big Foot. I was short for my age, and for years only my feet grew. Sometimes I could feel my toes reaching for the ends of my shoes. By the time I was in first grade, I wore a size six. My mother determined this was a sign. I would be tall, as tall as Aunt Greta, whose neck was so long, she reminded me of an ostrich. Men, my mother said, are intimidated by a tall woman, a woman like a tower whose head rises above the rest, unless she can carry herself with grace, like my aunt Greta who could balance a book on top of her head and eat lunch at the same time. I was forced to take ballet. It was strange enough walking on extra large feet, much less dancing on them. Sometimes, in ballet, I was benched. Every Thursday, on the way to class, I felt sick. My stomach ached. I winced from the pain, which angered my mother who admired strength. Men of machismo. Pillars of society. On the car ride home, she'd tell stories to inspire me, myths of brave girls and boys like the Spartan boy who kept a fox under his tunic. But the fox grew hungry and bit into the boy's skin, lapping his blood. The boy didn't flinch or gasp. *Did he live?* I asked. Oh yes, of course. He not only lived, he thrived. He grew up to become a great warrior, the greatest of his time.

No, I argued. *He did not. He died.* I knew he died. Still, I saw him, night after night, when I was falling asleep. I counted his soldiers, marching in perfect form, like the notes in a funeral dirge. The ones who complained kept foxes beneath their tunics. Until their guts were eaten, until they felt nothing, no hunger, no fear, no pain. These were my mother's dancers, the chosen ones, her beloved ballerinas of war.

Bathing in Your Brother's Bathwater

Bathing, Miss De Angelo informed us in health class,
is very important, especially once you become a teenager.
In fact I can smell many of you this very day,
so I advise every one of you girls
to go home and take a good long bath tonight.
I know some of your folks like to skimp on water,
but consider it homework.
Say Miss De Angelo assigned it to you.
But girls, let me warn you.
Never take a bath in the same water as your teenage brother.
Why?
Well picture this.
All those tiny bubbles settling on your legs
when you sit in a nice tub of water?
If you could count every itty, bitty bubble,
that would be only a fraction of how many sperm
stream from a single man.
Even if he doesn't touch himself,
the water does.
And it only takes one.
One fast-moving whip-tailed sperm.
And you know how easy it is to catch a cold,
how quickly that little virus races clear through you.
And once that happens,
no one will believe you're any Virgin Mary,
no matter what you say.

Southern Accent

The day I came home with a busted lip and two black eyes,
my mother said the problem with me
was my southern accent. *Get rid of that extra "y"*
in Dayaddy, and you're talking about your father,
not some deity.

I tried to tell her it began with a dayare,
but my mother said it was dare, not dayare,
and besides that, she didn't want to hear
one thing about it.
A girl is supposed to speak nicely.
And act like a lady.
If you're going to fight like a boy,
you can cut your hair like one, too.
What's more, that stuff growing on top of your head
is not hay as in hayer, it's hair.

Driving to Watson's Beauty Salon downtown
on Jefferson Park Avenue, she instructed me
to open my mouth nice and wide, say *ahhh*, not *ayyy*.
I didn't mean to, I tried to explain.
It was just an accident.
Not everything rhymes with Bayer, my mother commented.
She was from New England. She wasn't like me.

But I never could get it right. No matter how hard I tried,
I'd hear my father's voice,
his Memphis drawl in the back of my head:
You being about as helpful as a crawdayaddy under a rock?
When was the last time you peeled your mama spuds
or washed your hayands and said something sweet
with a smile on those rosebud liyips?

I knew how to answer him, keep my eyes cast down,
my voice a wisp: *No, sir. Yes sir.* Or, if I dared:
Can I please be excused?
No ma'am, he'd answer just as quick as a blink.
You can. But you may not.
Not as long as you don't know
which word is proper,
and what kind of excuse you might be.

I'd wait, keep my mouth shut tight.
But there were always those thoughts
circling my mind, sassing him like a beginner's violin,
the slow ache in the middle of each word
I'd never lose:

You think you're as bright as a rock
on a rain-soaked night?
When was the last time you were anybody's wish?
But my best one was this: *You say you're my daddy.*
Well, what if?

The Day Grandma Saw God

It happened on a day like any other day.
I'd been down at the pond,
catching crawdads in a bucket,
watching a chicken hawk
circle overhead.
Grandma was out in the orchard
picking fruit.
For lunch my mother served cold biscuits
and stew.
Grandma said she'd been out
gathering the pickling pears
when it happened.
The voice of God came through.
Lou, it said, *I'm calling home my faithful servant,*
old Miz Mason.
She looked up at the naked air
and saw the angels flocking like crows,
though to tell it honest,
she could hardly see
for the light blazing.
Mark my words, Grandma Lou sighed,
forking out another heap of tomato beef stew.
Miz Mason won't be long for this world.

Dad kept chewing his food.
My mother picked a daddy longlegs
off the magnolia blossom
and carried it outside.
No one paid Grandma much heed.
She always had a way
of forecasting doom,

knowing just who was dying
which week.
Said she could feel them
like minnows
slipping between her palms.

A day or two after Miz Mason passed on,
Grandma Lou and I sat out on the porch swing,
shucking corn and picking off earworms.
I asked her did she recollect
what the angels wore,
and if they played harps or dulcimers
like my mother did.
But Grandma said it looked like
she wasn't one
to see God's minions up close,
but it must be gobs of them up there,
sort of like bees on the moon.

In Grandma's Bathroom

Centipedes raced across the linoleum and scurried up the stone walls.
I stared into her cracked mirror and at the rows of empty perfume
bottles, dusting myself with her talcum powder and cologne. Her toilet
never stopped running. Grandma would come in and rattle the handle,
take the top off the tank, pull the black ball up in the back, and say
I wasn't supposed to be using her facilities anyways. As if her huge,
ancient behind made the porcelain seat unfit for my bony butt. One time
Grandma sat on the toilet seat and broke it in three pieces. Another time
I walked in and saw her, wrinkled and wet, rising up and up from the
bathtub like a genie from a bottle. There was so much of her, I couldn't
stop staring, wondering how it all fit in one tub, on one set of old bones.
She dried herself off with a floral tea towel, dabbing inside all her creases
and crevices. *Look here, honey child,* she said. *Don't you be slipping in
here again, hear?*

Snow White

1.

White stone, lifted from the sandbar off the coast of Pawleys Island,
surface smooth as a geisha's skin. What is it? I ask. A shoulder blade?
A kneecap? Always she turns her face away. Who can blame her after
sleeping for years in a glassy world, above her only green waves, sky,
gulls. *Did she hear them cry?*

2.

Did she dream? Was she an insomniac, too? My grandma didn't know,
or if she did, she never said. She always did leave the best parts out of
the fairy tales. *Hush. Get your beauty sleep now.* She'd pat my head
and slip away. Outside my window the moon glowed. That was the year
astronauts walked on it. Squinting, I wanted to see them take their first
steps, and ask if God was with them in the dark, the God who made
the gullies for the rain and the path for the thunderbolts and the moon.
I didn't like Him. He bossed and ruled so much, I held my breath. *Go
away,* I prayed. *Please. Go away.*

3.

Hovering above my grandma's bed, a pale ghost, I fingered her vials
of medicine, small white pills, her true loves, white as bone, white as
her powdered skin. *Wake up, wake up.* She never moved. I felt for her
breath, the pulse on the blue vein climbing her neck like a vine. Afraid, I
curled up beside her as close as I dared.

Gills

By the time I was in third grade, I could swim three lengths of an Olympic-sized pool underwater. I told my friends I had gills. I was fast, too, on account of the webbing that grew between my fingers and toes. I liked to show it off, make sure everyone said, *That's really gross.* In those days *gross* was a first-class compliment.

I never let on I was getting holier by the minute. But the minister always said, *We have a lot to learn from the dead. Let us follow the examples of those who have gone before us.* Like what? I wondered. I figured one thing for sure. The dead never took any breaths. So I started practicing.

Sometimes I'd come home from school and brag, *I breathed only fourteen times today.* Grandma would be busy doing something like whipping cream, and she'd just say *mmmhmm.* Of course I lost track, and maybe fourteen was all I counted, but I had to be special at something. I never did want to be just ordinary. My favorite word was EXTRA-ordinary, with the extra in all caps. Just thinking about my powers, I felt like a superhero. I'd challenge anyone to a contest. *Bet I can hold my breath longer than you can.*

That was before Tommy Malone took me on. It was a Monday in March, and Tommy had a freshly buzzed head. He said his new dad made him do it. Actually, he wasn't just buzzed. Tommy was bald. He had a new dad every year, and when we asked what his mama did, he said she didn't do anything. She just said yes. I tell you this because I want to explain. Tommy was strange. And I don't want to be blamed for what happened next. It was right in the middle of Mrs. Mullnex's spelling class when we started holding our noses. Mary Beth Wiley was referee. Pretty soon Tommy started to sweat. His head glowed like a red halo. I could have sworn it even smoked. For a moment, I thought he was going to explode. I was just about to say, *it's okay. You win,* when Tommy slumped over, slid clear off the side of his chair, and spread out onto the linoleum. His head hit the floor and bounced. His glasses broke, and the lenses popped out of the frames. Mrs. Mullnex waved her hands and bobbed back and forth like a bowling pin that was hit but not knocked down. I was so bad, the principal said that day, did I know I needed saving from the Lord, *Hisself?*

On the car ride home Grandma said what I did wasn't exactly wrong. Sitting beside me, the wipers going slap-slap, the rain gushing off her black Buick, she suggested I might want to start breathing again. That the dead don't, as I always imagined, stay underground. Instead they float up like mist in the spring. That's the way she pictured it anyhow. *You can't keep a soul down,* she informed me, *no matter how bad things get.* That's when I let my breath go. I let it glide out and out. It felt so good, leaving me, I could almost imagine myself ascending, rising along with it. Like the Lord, Mother Mary, and all the heavenly hosts. I wondered if one day I'd levitate. Make everyone clap.

Bzzzz

Dad watched me suck honey off my fingers, lick the spoon, and sink
it back in the Mason jar. Above me, dozens of flies clung to the sticky
paper swinging beneath the ceiling fan. I stared at their wings, thinner
than tissue. She'd almost been a mother to me, Dad said. No one could
have predicted this. What was I going to do now, without her to come
home to? I listened to the fan hum and asked, did he know that girl flies
have eyes spread apart while all the boys are cross-eyed? Had he seen
that fly up on the corner window with white powder like sugar under
its feet? Grandma said flies like that have caught a disease. That's why
they don't move. Look close and you can almost see the little granules.
But Dad just couldn't get over it. The other week Grandma was fixing
five zucchini pies. She never did give her recipe to Cousin Ada. Wasn't
it just like her, carrying her recipes to the grave? A fly buzzed above my
plate, danced its legs in honey, then sped off in sharp-angled turns. Dad
stared out the window, past the towels flapping on the line, almost as if
he were expecting Grandma to come strolling up the dirt path, red
suitcase in hand, the way she did that Saturday in Indian summer when
she announced, this time she was coming to stay.

What the Dead See

after Frank Stanford

Back then I never let on. Besides, no one was there to set the record
straight, the womb I fell from, soused with liquor. And there was any
kind of excuse. I was younger then than I ever knew, in air swimming
with insects. Sometimes, talking with the Baptist preacher on the patio
about the folks who have gone from this world, I felt them, like they were
fish bones caught in my throat. *The dead have things,* he'd say, *they
don't even let on to the devil they know. The living does too.* Like my
head was a transistor radio, he wanted to find that gospel station, make
me fear the Lord. His breath, warm on my face, a whiff of fish thawing,
the rain like small feet on the lake. I'd watch it and sip from a green
Coca-cola bottle slowly, wondering what the Lord and the devil don't
know, seeing nobody seeing us. Nights, when my folks came home late,
the headlights crossed my ceiling. Shadows kept falling and falling. I'd
watch my sister's boyfriend slip out. She was good at faking shit, like
sleep, like caring what she did. Afterwards, I'd listen. Sometimes the
dark would look at itself and sigh, and the wind would blow in the alfalfa
field. I'd hear someone whispering so soft, no one heard her words.

Part II

Calling the Snakes

Lying

Back then it was an art,
a way of closing up
all those tiny wounds,
taking the whole world inside
and letting it burn.

Nobody ever cared
to set the facts straight,
all those lies
trapped inside us
like a movie with no sound
we'd keep on living in
just as long as we could.

If anyone ever asked,
we said *yes'm* and *fine*
and *it sure is, thank you,*
or *pretty good,*

and after dinner
we'd ride our bikes
over to the DQ
for a frozen custard,

and lick in the dark,
let the breeze blow
through the peach trees overhead,
let our lips touch places
we'd say we'd never been.

Sundays

sitting beneath the fan in the kitchen,
the blade shadows going over
and over my face,
I listened to the gospel on the radio,
some Baptist preacher saying
it was high time
we learned to walk right
with the Lord. The sin
can seep from the body
like oil from a rusty can.

Wasps crawled over and over
the bruised plums in the bowl
on the kitchen table.
When the hymns began,
I picked burdock from my kneesocks
and hummed along.
Bobby Jones, the hired kid from town,
came up from the horse barn,
plucked a floating egg
from a jar of pickle juice
on the counter, the dirt
from his fingers rising
in a dark cloud.

We never said a word.
Afterwards, I watched him
head down the gravel road to the stalls,
his body-glide inside his clothes
like some kind of music
riding his skin.
I didn't want to let on
I was looking.
That's how much I liked him.

Hiring the One-Armed Man

After being in the military, I've done my time. Now I make my own rules, but I can work. Yes sir, I can. I can work a farm with one arm now that I got this new one from the V.A. Let me show it to you. Comes with its own attachments. Insert a knife, a fork, and a screwdriver if you want to. Now, I ask, who wants to wrestle a man with silverware for a hand? I'm as good as a fighting cock with fittings on his legs. I mean to say, I can really operate with this thing. And I can handle any kinda machinery you want me to. That much they taught me overseas. Mr. Maupin, they used to say about me, he can fix anything. And my son, Jimmy, he's a hard worker, too. Doesn't do a lick in school. Can't hardly read his own name. But give the boy a pitchfork or a shovel, and he'll sweat and haul like a man twice his age. He likes to show off, too. Sometimes I go out back for a cigarette, and I ask him to join me. Landsakes, boy, I say. Stop for a spell, why don't you? Have a smoke. But he don't. He just says, Yes sir, no sir, or I don't know, sir, and he keeps right on shoveling. So I teach him a thing or two. Like how to fish trout and hunt groundhog. Like how snakes smell in the hot July sunshine. He can sniff better than a hound dog, that boy can, and tell just when a rattler or copperhead is slipping around a barn. That way I make sure I raised him up good. So he knows what a fella can't see. Sort of like the arm I'm missing. It's always hanging by my side. When I reach out and touch folks with it, I feel a body just like he is. That way I always know what I'm dealing with.

Calling the Snakes

I know this story can't be true. But I remember it. Exactly. I can close
my eyes and see it. I'm eleven years old. I know this because it's my
birthday, and it's hot as Texas outside. Ninety-two degrees in the shade.
It's the first day I'm allowed to go barefoot all year. I have to ask permis-
sion from my dad who says it's never hot enough to take off your shoes.
Why? He's from Memphis. My mom hates the heat because she's from
Boston. I wonder if all marriages are like that. I think so, but that's not
what this story is about. Maybe it's not even a story. Maybe I just dreamt
it. To explain things, like why I don't like the number eleven. Two ones,
side by side, two skinny legs. Stilts, too awkward to walk on. Eleven.
Too old to be a kid, too young to be a woman. I still wear underpants
with the days of the week embroidered on each one. Seven pairs, seven
colors. My sister is fifteen, and she has a whole collection of pink
brassieres. My sister wants to go fishing over at Milton's pond, and she
says she will take me because it's my eleventh birthday. I know that's
not really why. She doesn't give a hoot about my birthday. Oh no. She
knows that if we fish, Jimmy will fish too. He will talk to me and glance
at her. *Me*, I want to say. *Look at me*. But he won't. He'll just brag. And
I don't want to be there, listening to Jimmy brag, listening to Jimmy tell
stories about Jimmy. Like the one about calling the snakes.

I don't believe it. I say, *You can't call any stupid snakes*. He says yes
he can, too, so I say, *Yeah? Go ahead. Prove it then*. And he does.
Sitting beside us on the bank of Milton's pond, looking at my sister, he
makes a strange noise with the back of his throat and grins. I think he's
just showing off. *Creep*, I say, and stare past him and out at the pond.
That's when I see them. Two water moccasins, side by side, a perfect
eleven, swimming. Jimmy sees them too, so he starts tossing pebbles in
their direction. They turn their heads. I see the glint off their eyes and
skins, the U-swirl in the water as they turn. The snakes head right for us
then, and they don't just stop at the water's edge. They slither up the
red clay bank, slipping over the stones as Jimmy sings snake tunes and

laughs until they come so close, he could pick them up. Then he pelts them with rocks. When they're almost dead, he slices their heads off with a pocket knife, but their bodies continue to dance in slow S waves. *Why?* I ask. *Why'd you do that?* Because there're two, he says. *One snake never comes by hisself.* I'm so mad, I want to punch him then, but my sister is shrieking and crying, putting on a big show so Jimmy will put his arm around her. And he does. They walk off across the meadow toward home, leaving me with the fishing gear and the dead snakes. I hear them laugh a little, and watch Jimmy lean his body into hers. Their faces glow in the late afternoon sun. That's the first time they kiss. I hate them then. I hate them both.

.

Elvis

Dad used to say, *most men are good-for-nothings,* but don't think about that. Think about the men who are good for something because you are where your thoughts are, and he was right. That's why I'm with Elvis so many nights. I can't help it. I've been with him so long, I feel him deep inside me like an ache or pang I can never get rid of.

I mean right now there's Elvis playing on the radio. He's singing gospel, and I'm remembering the first time I heard him sing. Dad played his album on the stereo. I was a girl, maybe five or six years old. Mom was out of town, so Dad fixed me a whiskey or two—sweet drinks, he called them—an inch of sugar with whiskey, water, and lemon on top. He said it would give me a cultured taste for booze, something important to have for the future, and anyway, he didn't like to drink alone, and I liked whiskey, as my dad said, just like an ant likes sugar. It was in my blood before I knew what it was, this feeling Dad called whiskey love, and I call Elvis, the two of us sipping cocktails together, loving it together, with him on the flowered couch, reading the paper, eating Triscuits, me cross-legged on the floor in front of the fan, letting the wind fool with my bangs, humming, and when my dad stopped reading, he announced, *This guy is great,* and he sang along, *Are you lonesome tonight?*

And I was. Suddenly I was so lonesome, I was drunk with it, lonesome for Elvis singing, and my dad, lonesome for the fan blowing in my face and the cicadas outside, and the tree frogs, lonesome for that dusk that was all around me, the daylight fading so fast, I knew nothing ever lasts, not him, not Elvis. I was so lonesome, I was afraid I'd bust. That's when I thought of Terrence. I had to do something, so I thought of Terrence Jones, this kid at school who gave me a black eye. And when I thought of him, Elvis went away, and so did my dad. And the urge to cry. It was nice. I knew everyone's good for something. Even Terrence. Because I couldn't be there with my mind in that place where lonesome stays. And Elvis sings long after he's dead, and my dad too, now that he's gone, he just croons, *Does your memory stray to a bright summer day?* And my heart fills with pain when he comes back again and again, oh yes it does, too, until I think of someone else, some guy who's a real asshole, and I think, at least he's good for something. Look on the bright side. They can't all be Elvis. Except when I close my eyes.

The day the cows got loose

my dad said he should have known better
than to hire some fella who all but said
he was done being told what to do.
No sir, Mr. Maupin liked to answer.
I don't care to.
But he was good at driving the tractor
and mending whatever broke.
Most days he stayed in the toolshed
and lied, saying he'd done all kinds of work
he'd never begun.

One Friday he didn't even bother coming to work.
By night he was sauntering around the barn,
kicking the dogs and cussing.
Where you been all day?
*Down in the hollow, fixing the barbed wire fence
like I asked you to?* my father asked him.
He could smell the liquor in the air.
You bet, Mr. Maupin said.
You closed the gate up after yourself? Dad asked.
I sure did. Locked it up tight.
They watched the horses suck water from the trough.
You better be damn sure, Dad said.
Mr. Maupin grinned like he always did.
Damn sure, he repeated.
You bet I am.

5 a.m. the next morning, the phone rang and rang.
Nobody else heard it at first
with all the fans in the house humming on high.
Ma'am? I heard the sheriff's voice.

I hate to wake you,
but it looks like every heifer you folks own
is out grazing the freeway.

All that morning we spent rounding up cattle.
The neighbors helped, and Jimmy too.
Mr. Maupin slept in.
Every gate on the farm
was swinging loose on its hinges.
My dad said he was too drunk to lift his head.
After that it was Jimmy who worked for us.
His daddy *took sick* and had to stay in the bed.
That's what Jimmy said.

Spring Fever

It's the smell that gets me every time,
lilacs, cut grass, sweat,
and the air like a haze
clinging to my skin
until it warps and aches me,
and I think of Jimmy asking,
Are you lonesome-ish?
And I am
twelve years old again,
wishing for a first kiss.
One, I say, *just one.*
All I want is a little drizzle
before the rain.

Death Wishes

1.

Some mornings when I don't water my plant,
her neck falls to one side. Her petals droop.
Lady, I mean to say,
I don't care if you mope till the sun goes down.
What do you want?
Nothing, she'll be telling me. *Nothing.*
A kind of grudge she holds close.
So I forget her. I forget everything
even when it's as close as the kitchen sink
where she can wet her leaves
and dainty white feet. No matter what I say
she'll keep sucking up the dirt.

2.

Easier to let it go, my dad always said
when my mother took up raising Cain.
A woman always wins in the long haul.
Watching my mother hurt was worse
than trying to run in my sleep
and sticking fast.
Fingers in my ears, I'd slip out,
the rusty hinges, a singing between us,
the fear stuck in my throat.
Back then I never knew what the fuss was about,
or why she'd curse the day she was born.

3.

Down at the barn, Jimmy was always forking
out manure or raking sawdust,
smoke spilling from his mouth.
Some days he'd howl like a coon hound

just to make me smirk
and ask things. Like:
*Shouldn't you be inside
helping your mama wash up?*

4.

Resting my head on a mossy stone
beneath the fruit trees, listening
to Jimmy mouth off,
and the katydids,
I'd count peaches, cross my arms
on my chest and let the insects
crawl on my bare legs.
That's how I practiced dying
and never coming back.

Pearls

I dreamt you kept a banjo
between your blue-jeaned legs,

and you were liking singing off-key.
One day you took me to the movies

just to glide your hand up my dress.
I went to the ladies room and never came back.

That night the banjo played so loud in my sleep,
I could hardly rest. I woke

to see your car fishtailing
across our grass. The next day

you sent me two strands of pearls
and some lamebrained excuse.

I wore those pearls for a week
around my neck.

By then everyone was talking about
what I was like in the sack.

Part III

Snake Bites

The night Jimmy shot the red fox

the whole house hummed like an electric wire.
The front door whined on its hinges,
so many coming and going.
I woke, snuck down the steps,
and curled into the couch
by the woodstove,
expecting my father to say,
What do you think you're doing out of bed?
He always was one to send me back
where I came from.
Before he could say a word,
Jimmy stopped shooting pool
and came over to ask did I play tiddlywinks
or blow tunes on a pop bottle.
He closed his fingers over my naked knees
like a cat's paw, and told just how
he had scoped out the fox
I'd watched each dawn.
I could almost see her then,
slipping through the fog
lifting off the swamp,
her mouth full of chicken,
her ears rising above the weeds
like small flames or wings
before vanishing into the shadows
her life depended on.

Boston Strangler

I never saw *Leave It to Beaver,* so the other day, when my friend Alice, mentioned June Cleaver, I thought she was talking about Eldridge Cleaver's mother. And when she said my husband used to look just like one of the Monkees, I told her I don't like comparing him to a zoo animal. I had no clue which *Lucy* episode she was mimicking when she pursed up her lips and sampled my vitamin syrup. "My dream was to be *That Girl,"* she explained, as if I knew which girl *that* was. "And I used to *live* for the box. I mean, where were you?"

But my parents never took us to the movies. And we didn't own a TV. I only watched it when I visited my aunt in Brookline, Mass. She watched *The F.B.I.* and *Lawrence Welk.* She told me the Boston Strangler was loose and had a special interest in small blonde girls walking alone in city streets. I looked for him everywhere we went, but she said he was probably in disguise, so he could be anyone, even the cabby or someone else pretending to be nice. She held my hand with her leather glove when we shopped, and she took me to see the opera, which was even worse than *Lawrence Welk.* I plugged my ears and fell asleep on her large black bag.

Back home, even at the barn, I imagined the strangler was following me down unlit streets. I'd race up the ladder to the loft and hide behind hay bales, watching mud daubers float between the rafters. Nights, my face pressed against the pillow, I'd listen to owls screech and picture him swooping through my window, taking whatever he pleased. I'd wonder if there were places to hide, like a rabbit in a thicket or minnows in deep water. If there were rooms to slide into and stay safe forever. I'd think about the agents on *The FBI,* driving down the dirt road, saying: "This is where she was last seen."

Bees

Nights my father walked the dirt path past the cow barns to the bees
he kept in cedar nests. There haven't been bees for years. That's how
old he was, but he never did stop lecturing me on how to select the
right kind of man. A honeybee, he always said, travels to the same
kind of flower. Why? Because a clover bee is meant for clover. I asked
if he knew if the bees slept, and if they slept, did they dream. I liked
orange blossom honey best. There were bees in our house, climbing the
screens. Wasps too. My dad caught them in a handkerchief and shook
them loose outside. Whenever I tried, I squeezed too tight and broke
off wings and legs. He always said I'd never learn. I was already a
woman, too full of fear and grab.

The year my sister turned fourteen

she'd get so bored
she'd watch the kitchen clock for hours,
the second hand sweeping the Roman numerals.
Outside the chickens squawked
and scuffled over scattered corn.
When she opened orange after orange,
the fine mist from the skins rose
in a fountain of tiny droplets.
I could almost taste the juice on my tongue,
but she never handed me a section.
These are my oranges, she said with a smirk.

Sometimes she went looking for Jimmy,
and mocked our father's words,
Don't you be hanging around that boy alone, hear?
Dressed in her cheerleading dress
with a red A for Albemarle High,
she didn't know yet she could be tossed
in the air as easily as salt.
Or why our father always tossed spilled salt
right hand over left shoulder for luck.
She was still young enough to dream
of a life beneath the floodlights,
her blonde hair floating overhead,
her body rising forever like an angel's.
Maybe that's why the farmhand said, *Nope,
Jimmy's not home, dear, but take a looky here.*

He lit moths on fire with his cigarette
lighter, just to show her
how easily wings can burn.

Adolescence

I never knew you then, though I remember that spring a squinty-eyed girl
kneeling on the gravel driveway in Virginia, fingering a frozen bee. The
bee had already passed out of the bee, you thought, but it stung anyhow,
in one last surge. The spine arcing into your hand, then curling up like
a child in a fetal position. You screamed, ran inside, the screen door
slamming behind you. That year you cried a lot, still pretending you
were Helen Keller, bumping into the sharp edges of tables and the kitchen
counter. The farmhand's son, your first crush, went steady with Sarah Lee
Combs, a waitress at HoJo's who wore miniskirts that showed more than
her legs. She liked to cook the turtles he caught in the pond by feeling in
the mud with his toes. Afternoons, listening to him say her name, *Sarah
Lee,* again and again, you imagined the moles on her hairless legs, her
scent of sweat and vanilla. You forgot your chores and what you were
saying mid-sentence. At school you stopped playing jacks with the other
girls at recess. One day you sat alone on the stone steps, eating a
tangerine, watching two boys bat a tetherball. Juice beaded on your
lips. Slowly, carefully, you bit into each section, savoring tiny mouthfuls,
spitting out the seeds. Fresh blood bled through a Band-Aid on your
thumb and leaked a crimson star on a segment of tangerine. You didn't
notice yet the taste of iron mixing with juice on your tongue.

Why Abortion Doesn't Make Sense

Catholics don't believe in abortion, Miss De Angelo said.
Even if it's true they multiply like rodents.
No matter what folks say about conception,
everyone knows.
If a woman gets pregnant,
it's not bunnies or snakes she's having or vice versa.
You don't need the pope to tell you that.

Summer

Sometimes in the middle of the day, Jimmy and I'd rest on the upside-down feed buckets beside the sugar maples, sip Cokes and talk about our dreams, maybe watch the horses slurp water and swish off gadflies. Jimmy talked about Sarah Lee, his girl (he liked to say so long after she wasn't). Then he would lie back with his ball cap over his face while I fished dead frogs out of the trough. I'd think about what it's like to be the girl every boy talks to about the girl he likes. Sometimes I watched him sleep until the lizards ran out to wait by the water for insects to light. If I wanted to, I'd pick off their tails and show them to Jimmy when he woke.

After the snake bit him

Jimmy liked showing off where the fangs went in. *You can't blame a gal when you grab her from behind,* he'd say. Like the snake had to be some kind of *gal.* I just smirked, tossed my ponytail, and walked away. That was the year I wouldn't muck stalls or toss horseshoes or listen to his talk about what he did with this girl or that. Instead I rode my fat-tired bicycle into town and had my hair permed in a thousand curls. All I ever cared about was how I looked. Like the night I dressed up in a polyester double knit dress that clung to my skin like bad weather. *Fine,* Jimmy said. *You look real fine.* Then he lit up a cigarette and blew smoke in the dark, like it meant nothing to him.

Dance Lessons

Sometimes, Jimmy said to me,
I don't know about you, girl.
I really don't. All those classes
your folks have you take,
like dancing.
I seen how you move, too, those long gowns
sliding across the floor,
like a fish, hooked and pulling wake,
then jerking every once in a while from side to side.
Personally I don't care for it.
Me, I just listen to String play banjo or guitar—
we call him String because he's skinny,
it's true, but also because he can pick a tune
on his strings any night
and set it loose in a man.
All you got to do, then,
is put your heels to the ground.
It's hard not to.

Whenever I asked

is Jimmy home,
his daddy said, *No'm,
I haven't seen hide nor hair
of that boy. Good thing.*
He'd be out by his pickup
cleaning his guns
or showing off.
He liked taking aim
at whatever moved.

Once he shot a kitten.
Other days he shot squirrels
and groundhogs.
But it was birds, he said,
he was fond of.
Because birds is the easy ones.
Once they spread their wings,
there's no trees or grass
to hide inside.
They're just targets
against an open sky.

I thought of this
years later
when Jimmy was shot
down over Vietnam.
He survived.
At least they say he did.

The last time I saw him,
he asked if I wasn't a sight

for sore eyes.
Then he showed me his fake
limbs.
He said that wasn't all
he was missing. And grinned
just like his daddy always did.

The Past

If she closed her eyes, she could see it
in the dark room of her mind,
the jukebox of her soul
developing so slowly,
she especially liked the way
he said the word, *blouse,*
when he unbuttoned her
silk blouse, blue blouse, flowered blouse,
his favorite one was pink
and hung on a green lamp
like a flower on a stem
now that he was gone,
and so was she
and no one lived there anymore,
the town kept lighting up without them
as if it were the first dusk.

Part IV

Strange Birds

Strange Birds

The year no one slept, the rooster crowed just about any hour of the
night. Dad named him No Doze, and if anyone ever asked what kind
of bird that was, he said he was a Delusional. Grandma thought he
said Andalusian. She was into pedigrees. She was sure No Doze was
some kind of exotic specimen. *All those overbred animals do peculiar
things,* she said. Some nights I imagined No Doze arriving by ship
from someplace in another time zone. Other times I thought weasels
were lurking around the coop. Jimmy said weasels were all over the
place, and they'd eat my chickens for a midnight snack any night. He
hadn't seen a coop yet that could keep weasels out. Once I ran through
the dark in my PJs, wanting to see one. But weasels are quick. *Footsteps
sound like thunder to weasels and snakes,* Jimmy said. *Shoot, they can
hear you roll over in the bed.*

But the night my dad stayed up waiting for Mazey, the mare, to foal,
that rooster almost drove him to the brink. By the time the vet came, it
was too late. The foal had died in utero. The vet just shook his head.
When birds act strange, he said, *it's a bad sign.* Grandma said she
should have known. She'd been suggesting for weeks that someone was
about to pass on. She just couldn't say who or what. By then Jimmy had
a thing for No Doze. *Give him a few years, why don't you?* he asked
my dad. *He's just a teenager in a house full of hens.*

But Dad didn't want to hear a word about it. He turned No Doze loose,
and the red fox picked him off in broad daylight. Jimmy said the rooster
just fell over, toes to the sky. Roosters do that. Their little chicken hearts
start beating so fast, they pass out cold. That way they never know when
death comes. But we all heard it late in the night. The silence of a farm
when nobody's crowing. Unable to sleep I stayed up listening. Grandma
said I'd best get used to it. That way I'd know when death was singing
to me.

Ghosts

Never believe what you can't see, my father liked to say. My father didn't see Jesus. But he saw ghosts. All the time. He said they were commonplace, not just some trick of the eyes. After a while, a person gets used to them. Sort of like houseflies and weather. One morning a ghost might be sitting at your kitchen table, while another is floating down the sidewalk, admiring the lilacs and lilies. Makes sense, he said. People aren't all that different from ghosts. Think about it. A man isn't just the fella you see. He's both his body and not his body. He's the man you know and the one you don't want to. Like those murderers you read about in the newspapers every day, who are just the loveliest neighbors a person could hope to meet. Like that Mr. Mosley over on Elm Street who grew prizewinning roses and was arrested for killing five boys. He used their bodies for compost. People never do like to look truth in the face. They prefer not to know it. Just because someone appears nice, or alive, doesn't mean he is. Lots of the living don't really live. So some of the dead don't die. They just keep coming back to hang around and tell us about yesterday, last year, or way back then, once upon a time, when they were football stars, war heroes, or dogwood queens. We were all really something back then, now weren't we?

Nonsense

I hope you don't believe all that nonsense
your father tells you, my mother said.
He's always making up tales about ghosts
and magic and his sixth sense.
How he had a premonition
before his brother, Dyl, passed on.
But you know he never tells the same story
the same way twice.
I try to correct him.
Reginald, I say, *that never happened.*
Kate, he answers back,
this is my story.
Have another drink
and listen to it.

Sometimes he says
behind every tale there's another tale.
That's the one he wants to tell.
But I think he just makes stuff up.

He thinks he can invent
another world.
One he might want to live in.
I ask, what if everyone did that?
He says most folks do.
Historians, palm readers,
lawyers, weathermen.
Politicians do it, too.
That's why we elect them.

If you want to learn how to eat properly

don't watch your father.
He chews with his mouth open.
If he doesn't like what he's chewing,
he spits it right out.
I hope you haven't noticed this fact.

If that's not bad enough,
your father has no *off* button.
Reginald, I say to him,
don't you think you should stop eating
once in a while?
He doesn't answer me.
He just takes another slice of pie.
Then he asks for the ice cream.

It's no surprise he got stuck in that rocker
down at the beach cottage.
He was all by himself
without a single person
to call for help.
I told him he could have died like that.
But he just scoffed
and said what he always says.
Someday, Kate, you'll read
about me in the newspapers:
Man Dies Due to Extra Large Behind.

Uncle Dyl's Ghost

All winter long I'd been grieving
the death of my brother, Dyl,
my father said.
It came as such a terrible shock.

Every time I thought about him,
I felt this pang deep inside.
I'd eat a little sweet to ease my mind.
Your mother tried to make me stop.
Reginald, she'd say,
now don't you think that's enough?

You know how Kate is.
She never understands.
She doesn't know how bad a pain can be,
how it can set into your bones,
and into that space at the back of your throat
where the air catches a little
before it lets you loose.

What's the matter with you?
she'd ask again and again.
But I didn't want to talk about it.
I just wanted to eat something nice.

By the time the weather had changed,
I'd had enough of Kate
and winter, too.
I needed to be alone.

I drove down to the beach cottage
where Dyl and I played as boys
and took long walks

with the wind and the waves.
I even did some spring-cleaning,
a little washing and scrubbing.

After two days of that,
I was so tired, I was wrung out
like an old dishcloth.
I decided to rest for a spell
in the wicker rocker
out on the patio.
But a terrible thing happened.

I tried to stand up
and that chair clung to my backside.
Next thing I knew,
I was pinned to the ground
like a turtle under its shell.
I didn't know if I'd ever get up.

But do you know, at that very instant,
a man appeared. Oh yes he did, too.
Out of nowhere. A man in a gray suit,
just like the one your uncle Dyl wore to the grave,
and he had on the nicest pair of white shoes.

I said, *Help me, sir. Please help me!*
He touched that chair, and off it slid
like a glove off a hand.
When I turned around to say *Thank you,*
thank you so much,
there wasn't a soul on the premises.

M

On the eve of his eightieth birthday, my father sat outside on the porch, sipping Jack Daniels, and said you know a man has one foot in the grave when he's nostalgic for the life he never lived. Like it's some sort of woman he never loved. That night he admitted there had been another woman once. She was the only woman he'd ever seen in the buff. *Your mother and me,* he explained, *we always shut the light off. But this was the middle of the day. I could see everything. Every freckle, mole, and hair on her body.* The sight scared him half to death. After she left, she said she wasn't ever coming back, but she promised she'd love him forever. And he promised himself never to say her name aloud. Now for the life of him he couldn't recall what it was. He only knew it began with M. It wasn't Mary Rose or Margaret or Mildred or Matilda. Or Melanie, Melissa, or Maude. Or Madeline or Michelle. He developed the habit of simply referring to her as M, and recently he couldn't help noticing how many Ms had died. It was sad to see them go. Almost like a flock of birds in fall. That's just how it happens, he sighed. One day we rise up from our skins, moles and all. And we're off.

Obituaries

The only section of the newspaper my father read was the obituaries. When he was too blind to read, I read them for him. He wanted news of any dead women whose names began with M. Like that Missy Ellen who lived on Walnut Street and passed away of unknown causes in her sleep, or May Dee Rawley, who died of a sudden heart attack. May Dee never once missed a game of Wednesday night Bingo. Or Margaret Lane, an avid bowler, who was in fine form until a cement truck struck her down on Buckingham Circle. But the one who really caught his attention was Maureen Pierce, survived by her sister, Betty. Maureen, I read, will always be remembered for her homemade butter biscuits and lemon meringue pies. Maybe her name *was* Maureen, he said. Yep, Maureen. That sounded right. I really miss her. Honest to God. And she did have a younger sister, and she could bake a mean pie, only it was rhubarb in those days. He said it made him sad to think that Maureen could have died before him. He could still see the way she pressed the piecrusts into the tins. The way her fingers felt on his skin, and he could almost taste the sweetness, too. It made him hungry just to think about it.

Maureen

Maureen never did die. I wouldn't allow it. Instead she kept right on living. And loving my dad forever, just like she promised she would. Of course she tried not to. We all did. And she always remembered the last time she saw him. It was fifty-five years ago if it was a day. I remember it, too, from the tidbits my father said. How he was walking down Elm Street in a hard rain, his red slicker pulled over his head, his trousers stuck against his thighs. He was crying, but he wouldn't turn around when she called his name. She knew he was sobbing even though she couldn't see his face. Maybe she wanted to stop but kept right on driving, the wipers going swish-swish, a Mozart sonata playing on WTJU. Afterward, whenever she heard Mozart, she was overwhelmed by pangs of grief or longing, she couldn't say which. It always made her think of what might have been. It's awful the way a memory feels when it won't leave a woman. Like something that keeps melting inside her, again and again, like little pats of butter in a hot skillet, no matter how often she tries to turn the heat setting down.

Something Else

Sometimes you say I'm *something else,*
and you mean I'm good, really good,
but honey, don't say that, please?
Reminds me how my dad used to say,
I'm just not myself today.
As if he were some kind of imposter dad.
Then he'd ask things like:
Why don't you go play with James?
Has the dog had his walk yet?
Will you kindly get out of my cotton-pickin' hair?
Sometimes he'd come home from work
carrying his hat and a brown paper bag,
and I'd know he wasn't my dad.
There were at least three daddies then,
sort of like daddy A, B, and C.
Like that TV show. Which will it be,
bachelor number 1, 2, or 3?
My mom often said he wasn't the man
she married. And I thought about that.
How, when they married,
I wasn't me, either. I wasn't anyone.
I didn't like to dwell on that.
It kind of gave me the creeps,
but I liked to ask,
Were you really in love then?
Of course, she'd say.
Did you hold hands?
Yes.
Kiss in public? Sit on his lap?
Yes, yes, I did all that. Once.
She even showed me photos
she kept in her lingerie drawer

beneath her slips and silky things
she never wore anymore: him
in his spats and slick-shined hair,
her in a pink crinoline cocktail dress
with her long bangs clipped back
in pearly barrettes. Not a thought
in her head, except maybe
Don't I look swell? And
Love me. And he did.
Did he say so?
He said it every day.
He was something else back then.

The Fight

It happened the morning my father reached for his shaving cream and knocked over my mother's $105-an-ounce Christian Dior Diorissimo perfume. Instead of apologizing, my father screamed a stream of profanities, so long and loud, even the three family hounds and four stray cats would not reenter the house for a week. That day my father told everyone, including the plumber and the druggist, that he couldn't comprehend how a sane soul could live with a woman whose bathroom is nothing but a maze of perfumes, powders, lotions, elixirs, pills, douches, palliatives, and God only knows what all else, and he kept right on talking, too, because it soon became clear that even after frequent laundering and dry cleanings, his favorite suit would forever retain the disturbingly floral scent he associated with both my mother and funeral parlors.

My mother had an instinct for retaliation. She began to inquire of guests at cocktail parties just why it is a man can't learn to control his aim. After twelve years of marriage, not a morning had passed, she explained, when she had not had to Lysol and wipe up at least one splash from the rim of her toilet bowl or floor. Long ago she had had to dispose of her lavender furry toilet covers and bath rugs. Surely they are unsanitary in any bathroom shared by the male species. She even began to wonder why some sort of disposable funnel had not been invented by Procter & Gamble or Johnson & Johnson, which could be attached to a penis, perhaps with a rubber band or Velcro, and made to conduct the flow neatly into a toilet bowl without mishap. Of course, she reasoned, men run the business world, and while they have no problem inventing any number of products to inhibit female odors and comfort, it would never occur to them to improve their own standards of hygiene, now would it? My mother even went so far as to design a hoselike mechanism, using the tubing from her defunct bonnet hair dryer for my father to "test-drive," but when he refused, she place a sign on the door, *Women Only*, and asked him to use the hall bathroom. In a house of many daughters, the message was clear. My father was not welcome.

Bee God

Men are like that, Mom used to say. They can't laugh or fake it on cue. Or act as if everything's fine, thank you very much. Some days I can't either. Like last night, I tried writing an elegy for my dad. A therapist suggested it might help with the grieving, recalling all the nice times. I tried. Honest I did. Then I gave up and started cleaning the house, sweeping dead bees from the window sills, fingering their wings, remembering the day I saw my dad covered with bees.

It was spring, and the queen must have just arrived. I was only six, and I wanted to scream, but I was afraid the bees would hear me and sting him. I didn't know if bees could hear, but I thought, with all that buzzing they do, they might. But the bees never stung my dad. He kept them in wooden hives behind the chicken coop. Sometimes at night the bees would fly into our house through the broken screens and bop around the lights, and he would catch them in a napkin, hold them gently, then shake them loose outside. My father liked to say that he was god of the bees, saving their lives and setting them free. That's what I do best, he'd laugh. *I, bee god.*

Southern Comfort

Whiskey on the rocks. That was my dad's evening drink. As a girl, I liked to hold my father's glass, feel the cold against my face, then lift it up so I could see the light coming through the liquid, golden like the hairs on my father's arms, like Triscuits and the meadow that stretched out behind the barn. Sometimes I'd sip it, and if Mom was out of town, Dad would serve me my own drink, mixing lemon, sugar, whiskey and water, letting me taste the fire on my tongue, throat, and deep inside. *Does it burn you, Daddy?* No, he'd say. Not with just one drink. Then he'd pour himself another one *to take the edge off the day*. And I'd watch it happen, the edges of the day dissolving, everything that had been the day moving away from us, no longer true or obvious like the black and white of the clock hands moving toward bedtime. When at last it was dark and late, and all that was left were two pools of lamplight, tiny 40-watt islands, just for us, my father reading on the couch, me on my belly, head cocked sideways, staring at picture books I'd read a thousand times, I'd play a game in my mind, trying to hold on to that moment, make it last, just a little longer, and pretend, this is all there is. Just this, this whiskey light, the two of us alone, together, on a summer night.

ACKNOWLEDGMENTS

I would like to thank the readers, editors, and publishers of the publications in which the following poems appeared:

ACM: "Adolescence"

Artful Dodge: "Calling the Snakes," "The Fight," "Ghosts"

Black Warrior Review: "Sundays"

Crab Orchard Review: "Southern Accent"

Cream City: "Snow White," "Boston Strangler"

Double Room: "What the Dead See"

Emrys Journal: "Summer," "Death Wishes"

Green Mountain Review: "Gills"

The Journal: "Being Mean"

MiOpoesis: "Powerful Magic," "Bees," "Bee God"

The Paris Review: "Bathing in Your Brother's Bathwater," "Why Abortion Doesn't Make Sense"

Poet Lore: "Lying," "The year my sister turned fourteen," "The Past"

The Best of the Prose Poem: "In Grandma's Bathroom"

The Prose Poem: "The Day Auntie Lou Saw God"

Sentence, Poetry Daily, The Alhambra Poetry Calendar 2008: "Southern Comfort"

"What the Dead See," *"Cleanliness is next to godliness,"* "Gills," "Being Mean," "Snow White," "The Day Grandma Saw God," "Bzzzz," "The night Jimmy shot the red fox," "Hiring the One-Armed Man," "The day the cows got loose," "Sundays," "Dance Lessons," "Strange Birds," and "Pearls" appeared in the chapbook *Any Kind of Excuse* (Kent State University Press, 2003).

"What the Dead See," and "The Day Grandma Saw God" appeared in *The Next of Us Is About to Be Born* (Kent State University Press, 2009).

OTHER BOOKS IN THE NOTABLE VOICES SERIES

Losing Season, Jack Ridl
Without Wings, Laurie Lamon
An Apron Full of Beans, Sam Cornish
The Red Canoe: Love in Its Making, Joan Cusack Handler
Bear, Karen Chase
The Poetry Life: Ten Stories, Baron Wormser
Fun Being Me, Jack Wiler
Common Life, Robert Cording
The Origins of Tragedy & other poems, Kenneth Rosen
Against Consolation, Robert Cording
Apparition Hill, Mary Ruefle

CAVANKERRY'S MISSION

Through publishing and programming, CavanKerry Press connects communities of writers with communities of readers. We publish poetry that reaches from the page to include the reader, by the finest new and established contemporary writers. Our programming brings our books and our poets to people where they live, cultivating new audiences and nourishing established ones.

CavanKerry now uses only recycled paper in its book production. Printing this book on 30% PCW and FSC certified paper saved 2 trees, 1 million BTUs of energy, 127 lbs. of CO_2, 67 lbs. of solid waste, and 524 gallons of water.